level

1

READERS

Snakes
Alive!

Louise P. Carroll

KINGFISHER

First published 2012 by Kingfisher
an imprint of Macmillan Children's Books
a division of Macmillan Publishers Limited
20 New Wharf Road, London N1 9RR
Basingstoke and Oxford
Associated companies throughout the world
www.panmacmillan.com

Series editor: Heather Morris
Literacy consultant: Hilary Horton

ISBN: 978-0-7534-3320-1
Copyright © Macmillan Publishers Ltd 2012

9 8 7 6 5 4 3 2 1

1TR/1011/WKT/UNTD/105MA

A CIP catalogue record for this book is available from the British Library.

Printed in China

Picture credits
The Publisher would like to thank the following for permission to reproduce their material.
Every care has been taken to trace copyright holders. However, if there have been unintentional
omissions or failure to trace copyright holders, we apologize and will, if informed, endeavour
to make corrections in any future edition.
Top = t; Bottom = b; Centre = c; Left = l; Right = r
Cover Shutterstock/Eric Isselee; Pages 3 Shutterstock/Matthew W. Keefe; 4 Frank Lane Picture
Agency (FLPA)/Michael & Patricia Fogden/Minden; 5 Photolibrary/OSF; 6–7 Shutterstock/
Kruglov_Orda; 7 Shutterstock/J.J. Morales; 8 FLPA/Michael & Patricia Fogden/Minden;
9 Photolibrary/Animals Animals; 10–11 Shutterstock/Ryan M. Bolton; 12–13 Photolibrary/John
Cancalosi; 14–15 FLPA/Dietmar Nill/Minden; 16 FLPA; 17 KF Artbank; 18 & 19 Naturepl/ Kim
Taylor; 20–21 FLPA/Michael & Patricia Fogden/Minden; 22 Shutterstock/EcoPrint;
23 Shutterstock/Audrey Snider-Bell; 23 Shutterstock/Steve Byland; 23 Shutterstock/clkgtr37;
24 Photolibrary/Digital Vision; 25 FLPA/ Danny Ellinger/Minden; 26 Photolibrary/F1 Online;
27 FLPA/David Hosking; 28 FLPA/Heidi & Hans-Jurgen Koch/Minden; 29 Photolibrary/Alaska
Stock; 30–31 Shutterstock/erlire74.

A snake has no arms or legs.
But it moves along!

This snake climbs up a tree.

Up it goes!

4

This snake slides across
the sand.

It moves sideways and forwards.

A snake's skin has strong **scales**.

How does the skin feel?

It feels cool and dry.

Snakes come in all sizes.

This is one of the longest snakes.

python

This is one of the smallest snakes.

thread snake

Most snakes live
where it is warm.

The sun warms a snake's body.

A snake's tongue moves
in and out of its mouth.

A snake's tongue is like a nose.

It smells the air to find out
if food is near.

Snakes hunt for food.
They eat other animals.

An animal that is hunted
is called **prey**.

Snakes swallow
their food whole.

Most snakes eat their
prey alive.

Many snakes kill their prey.

Some wind around it and crush it.

Other snakes use **venom** to kill their prey.

When the snake bites its prey, venom comes out of its teeth.

These teeth are called **fangs**.

Some snakes eat the
eggs of other animals.

The snake
swallows
the egg.

It cracks
the shell.

Then it
spits the
shell out.

19

Some animals eat snakes.

Snakes have ways to stay safe.

A snake's colours can
help it hide.

Can you find the snake?

Hiss!

A snake hisses to scare away an animal that wants to eat it.

Some snakes have a **rattle**
in their tail.

They shake the rattle to scare
other animals away.

Some snakes spit venom.

Some snakes play dead!

Many snakes lay eggs.

The eggs **hatch** and
the baby snakes **slither** out.

Some snakes have live young.

The baby snakes slither off straight away.

A snake grows all its life.

It grows too big for its skin.

The old skin comes off.

New skin is underneath.

A snake leaves its old skin behind.

Then it moves along!

Glossary

fangs sharp teeth that inject venom

hatch when an egg cracks and a baby animal is ready to come out

hiss a sound a snake makes to scare away other animals

prey animals that are hunted and eaten by other animals

rattle the part of a rattlesnake's tail that can make noise

scales tough, plate-like skin covering a snake's body

slither the way a snake moves

venom a poison that some animals make to kill other animals